To ANDREW

For being good.

MERRY CHRISTMAS!

From GRANDMA.

XXX

It was a crisp Christmas Eve and Santa and his reindeers were busy delivering presents to all the good boys and girls.

Santa's sleigh ZOOMED over houses, twisting and turning silently through the snowy night sky. Santa squeezed down and up and up and down chimneys, carefully and quietly delivering lots of presents.

All was going to plan until he reached the second to last house on his list.

Suddenly, Santa noticed one of the presents was **missing**!

The reindeer looked in Santa's sack, they **searched everywhere** but the present was nowhere to be found!

"Oh no!" exclaimed Santa. "It must have fallen off the **sleigh**!"

Santa wondered what to do.
He had no time to look for the present but he didn't want to disappoint anyone on his Christmas list.

Then Santa had a FANTASTIC idea!

He looked at his delivery map to see where they were.
Then he checked his list to see who had been naughty or nice.

At the very
top of the list was .ANDREW.
So Santa and Blitzen (the smallest of
all the reindeer) squeezed
down the chimney...

...and crept quietly into his bedroom.

ANDREW yawned, stretched and rubbed his eyes. He thought he was still **dreaming** until Blitzen licked his face with his long, wet, pink tongue – YUCK!

"I need your help!" boomed Santa. He explained that a present had fallen off the sleigh and Santa wanted ANDREW to go with Blitzen to find it.

ANDREW, of course was VERY happy to help.

It was cold and snowy outside so ANDREW put on his warmest hat and long, stripy scarf.

ANDREW and Blitzen looked through Santa's telescope.

They looked down past the houses and through the trees, trying to find the lost present.

Suddenly they spotted it, sitting on top of a pile of snow at the bottom of a big hill.

He jumped on Blitzen's back and gave him a friendly pat and little tickle behind his fluffy ears.
Then with a gentle nudge they flew high into the starry night sky.

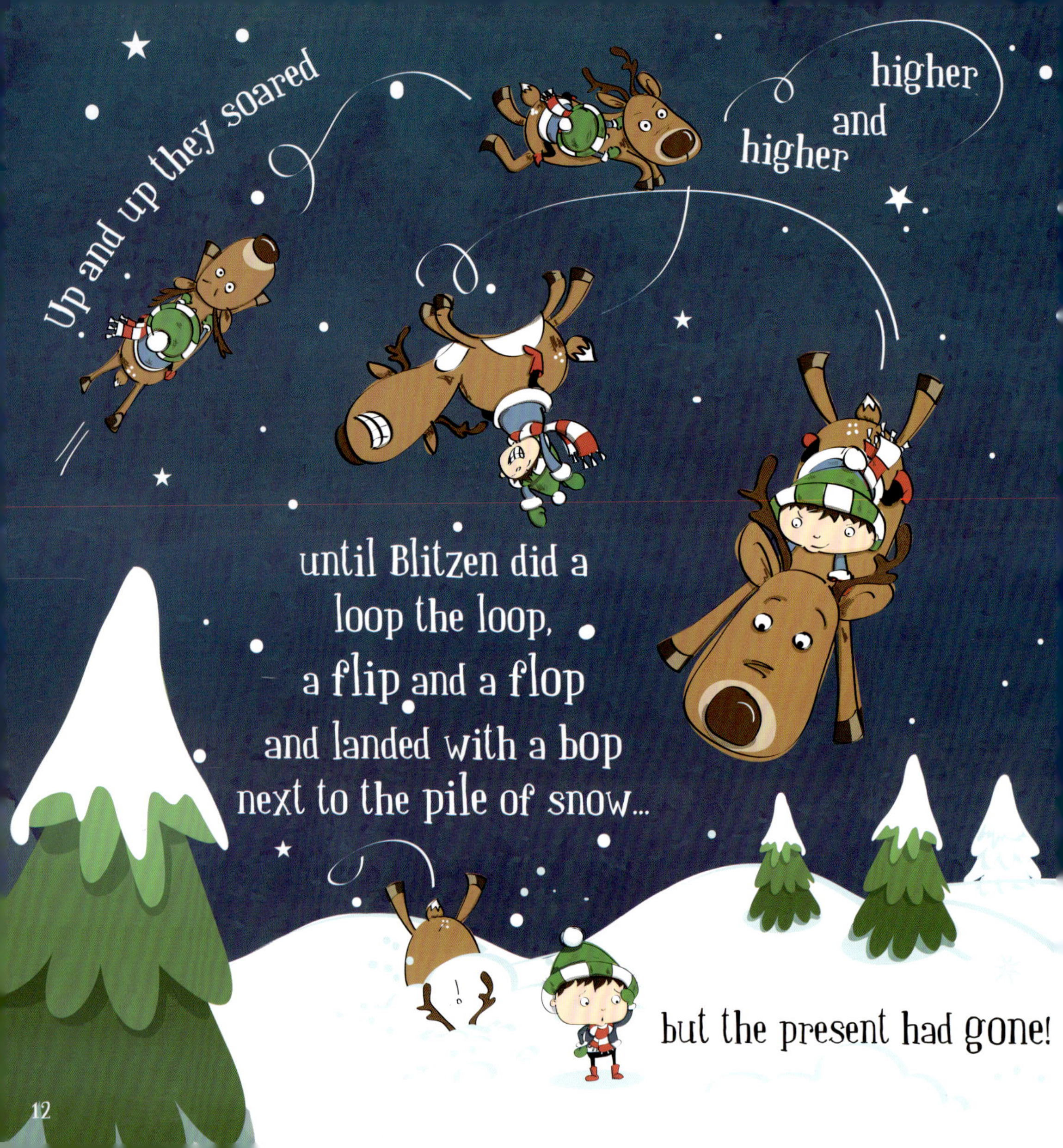

Up and up they soared

higher and higher

until Blitzen did a
loop the loop,
a flip and a flop
and landed with a bop
next to the pile of snow...

but the present had gone!

ANDREW ..and Blitzen looked around but couldn't see the present anywhere!

All of a sudden Blitzen's wet nose began to twitch and itch and wibble and wobble. What had he found?

ANDREW ..saw a bright orange carrot sticking out of the snow. "Who likes carrots?" he wondered. Perhaps this was a clue to where the present had gone.

Then they saw a tiny white and grey bunny rabbit.

"Hello Mrs Rabbit, we're looking for a missing gift which fell from Santa's sleigh. Have you seen anything?"

The bunny twitched her nose, rubbed her ears and pointed a fluffy white paw at a line of acorns.

"Who likes acorns?" wondered ANDREW.

Then looking down, they noticed a
bouncy red squirrel staring back at them.
They followed him, picking up the **acorns** one by one,
not knowing who or what would be at the end of the trail.

As they picked up the final acorn, they noticed a nose-less, button-less, very sad snowman right in front of them.

His carrot nose had fallen off and his acorn buttons had been lost but there, poking out from under his black hat, was a shiny Christmas present!

Hurray, they had found the present... but why did the snowman have it?

The sad snowman explained that every year he felt forgotten as he never received a present. When he found this one he was so happy. However, now he knew it belonged to someone else, he wanted to give it back.

Feeling sorry for the snowman, ANDREW decided to help.
He placed the half-eaten carrot on the snowman's face for his nose and the acorn buttons on his body - but the snowman still looked sad.

Then ANDREW had a brilliant idea!

He undid his fluffy scarf and tied it around the surprised snowman.

Then he replaced the snowman's old black hat with his warm knitted one.

The snowman was so happy! At last he had his very OWN Christmas present!

ANDREW and Blitzen flew as fast as they could to get the missing present back in time for Christmas morning.

ANDREW placed the gift under the tree with a huge sigh of relief!

Back at home ANDREW gave Blitzen a big hug, then watched as his new friend flew up into the sky and home to Santa.

When . . . .
woke up on
Christmas morning,
he wondered if it
had all been a dream.
Then he looked out
of his window...

...and there in the
distance was the happy
snowman waving at
him and he was still
wearing his lovely
Christmas present.

The end